Colin Powell

by Jill C. Wheeler

visit us at
www.abdopub.com

Published by ABDO & Daughters, an imprint of ABDO
Publishing Company, 4940 Viking Drive, Suite 622, Edina,
Minnesota 55435. Copyright ©2002 by Abdo Consulting
Group, Inc. International copyrights reserved in all countries.
No part of this book may be reproduced in any form without
written permission from the publisher.

Printed in the United States.

Edited by Paul Joseph
Graphic Design: John Hamilton
Cover Design: Mighty Media
Interior Photos: AP/Photo, p. 5, 6, 7, 9, 10
Corbis, p. 1, 13, 17, 23, 25, 27, 29, 31, 33, 34, 35, 37, 39, 41, 45,
47, 49, 51, 53, 55, 57, 59
Digital Stock, p. 14, 19, 20, 54
John Hamilton, p. 43
White House, p. 59

Library of Congress Cataloging-in-Publication Data

Wheeler, Jill C., 1964-
    Colin Powell / Jill C. Wheeler
        p.   cm. — (Breaking Barriers)
    Includes index.
    Summary: Describes the life of this American statesman, from his
birth in Harlem, to his role as general in the Persian Gulf War, to his
current position of secretary of state.
    ISBN 1-57765-638-5
    1. Powell, Colin L.—Juvenile literature. 2. Statesmen—United
States—Biography—Juvenile literature. 3. Generals—United States—
Biography—Juvenile literature. 4. African American generals—
Biography—Juvenile literature. 5. United States. Army—Biography—
Juvenile literature. [1. Powell, Colin L. 2. Statesmen. 3. Generals.
4. African Americans—Biography.] I. Title.

E840.8.P64 W48 2002
327.73'0092—dc21
[B]

2001027934

Contents

American Hero

*T*he 2000 United States presidential election was one for the record books. A month after Americans went to the polls, there still was no clear winner. Teams for Al Gore and George W. Bush each sought a victory through lawsuits and courtroom battles. Finally in mid-December, Gore conceded the race. Now President-elect George W. Bush faced a divided nation.

One of Bush's first jobs was to name his cabinet members. The 14-member cabinet is the primary advisory board for the president. The cabinet advises the president and his executive office on key matters involving everything from national security to transportation and housing.

One of the most important positions on the cabinet is the secretary of state. It is the highest-ranking position on the cabinet. The secretary of state advises the president on foreign affairs. For Bush, the choice was an easy one. He named retired Army four-star General Colin Powell as his choice. Bush said Powell was "an American hero, an American example, and a great American story."

Colin Powell with President George W. Bush.

With that nomination, Colin entered the history books again. He was to become the United States' first African-American secretary of state.

Colin's confirmation as secretary of state sailed through the required congressional approvals. It was as expected. In a divided nation, Colin was popular on both sides. Virtually everyone respected and admired him for his integrity, character, and ability.

Chairman of the Joint Chiefs of Staff Colin Powell at a press conference in 1993.

Colin Powell

As President-elect Bush had said, Colin's story is an example of the best America has to offer. The child of poor immigrants, he rose to leadership positions unheard of for African Americans. Some people even tried to draft him for president.

For some, such a taste of power would have led to a hunger for more. Colin has never been that way. Despite a resume with amazing accomplishments, he's still a down-to-earth man. When not advising on matters of national security or foreign policy, he still enjoys tinkering with Volvo cars and eating peanut butter sandwiches.

Bronx Boyhood

*C*olin Luther Powell was born on April 5, 1937, in Harlem, New York. Harlem is a neighborhood in New York City. In those days, Harlem was home to many immigrants. Immigrants are people who have moved from their home country to a new country.

Powell's family had moved to the United States from Jamaica. His father, Luther Theophilus Powell, had worked in a store in Jamaica. His family didn't have much money, so he had to work instead of finishing high school. He knew there was no future for him at the store. The 5'2" (1.8m) man took a job on a fruit boat and worked his way to the United States.

Powell's mother was Maud Ariel McKoy. She also was from Jamaica. She arrived in the United States to join other members of her family. Arie, as her family called her, had a high school diploma. Luther and Arie met at a church picnic and were married in 1929.

Like their neighbors, the Powells had little money. Few people did. The United States was just coming out of the Great Depression. Jobs were scarce, especially for immigrants and people of color. Luther succeeded through sheer hard work. He worked virtually every day in the shipping department of a clothing manufacturing company. He rarely got home before 7:00 in the evening. Arie worked as a seamstress. She put buttons and trim on women's clothing. For each piece she sewed, she had a tag. At day's end, she bundled the tags together. The company paid her for each tag. Together they made about $100 a week. In 1931, Luther and Arie had their first child, Marilyn.

Kids play a game of cards on the streets of New York.

The Manhattan skyline looms over tenement housing projects in 1939.

After Colin was born, the Powells eventually moved to an apartment in the South Bronx. "What many people now call a slum was a tenement neighborhood and a neat place to grow up when I was a boy," Colin said later. The Powells lived side-by-side with people from many different ethnic groups. There were Italians, Jews, African Americans, and Eastern European immigrants.

Colin enjoyed a happy childhood in the South Bronx. There was always some kind of game going on outside. He played in the streets with neighbor children of all colors. "Everybody was a minority," Colin recalled. "I did not know what a majority was."

Colin also loved to walk around the neighborhood. He enjoyed the different smells coming from the Jewish bakery, the Puerto Rican grocery store, and others. When he had a quarter to spare, he and his friends would watch cowboy movies at the local theater. He also loved serving as an acolyte at the family's Episcopal church, St. Margaret's.

At home, the Powell house was open to everyone. Many people respected Luther Powell. They looked to the couple for advice. Colin grew up knowing his family loved him very much. He also knew they had high expectations for him. He would live his life based on the values and code of honor that his family gave to him at a young age.

Just an Average Student

*C*olin attended public school in New York. He started at Public School 39. Then he attended Junior High School 52. Both schools were in his neighborhood. Colin did not excel in school. His grades were usually average or below average. "I lacked drive, not ability," he said. Meanwhile his sister Margaret excelled in school.

By the time Colin entered junior high, things in the Bronx were beginning to change. Colin's school was an example. It was an all-boys school, and it was tough. Rumor had it the principal walked around with a pistol. As an adult, Colin recalled what had happened to his formerly happy neighborhood. "We had lots of drugs in my neighborhood. On every street corner was some... junkie trying to sell or deal or get others involved in it."

Colin refused to try drugs. His family had raised him to respect his life. He knew drugs would damage that life. However, that doesn't mean Colin was perfect. When he was 13, he attended a church camp outside of New York City. It was an honor for him to

Colin didn't excel in school, but it was from a lack of drive, not ability.

attend the camp. Unfortunately, Colin fell in with a group of boys who wanted to make mischief.

One night, they smuggled beer into the camp even though they were too young to drink. They didn't think anyone would catch them. They were wrong. The priest in charge of the church camp found out. He asked who had brought in the beer. At first, no one answered. Then Colin came forward. "Father, I did it," he said. He was sent home in shame and had to face his family. They were very disappointed in what he had done. However, they respected that he had stepped forward to tell the truth. His bravery had helped some of the other boys admit that they had done the wrong thing, too.

Colin attended high school at Morris High School. At age 14, he also took a job working at a local store that sold baby furniture. He put furniture together, boxed furniture that needed to be shipped, and helped create store displays. He worked up to 15 hours a week for about 75 cents an hour.

Colin kept his job at the furniture store while attending the City College of New York.

Colin graduated from high school in February 1954 with a C average. By that time his sister Margaret already had graduated from Buffalo State College. Neither of Colin's parents had been able to attend college. However, they wanted their children to have that opportunity. They believed a college education was key to a successful future.

"I went to college for a single reason," Colin said. "My parents expected it." Colin narrowed his college choices to two. He applied to New York University (NYU) and the City College of New York (CCNY). Both colleges accepted him. Yet tuition at NYU cost $750 a year. Tuition at CCNY cost $100 a year. The choice was simple.

Colin enrolled at CCNY as an engineering major. His mother had told him engineering was where the money was. He began to commute to college so he could live at home. He also kept his job at the furniture store.

At first, Colin found college uninteresting. He did not like his engineering classes. Yet he didn't know exactly what he wanted to do. After a tough first semester, he changed majors from engineering to geology. He liked geology a little better. He told his parents he could use a geology education to work for an oil company. But finally he found something that truly captured his attention.

A Place in This World

*W*hile at City College of New York, Colin noticed many young men on campus in uniforms. He learned that they were members of the Army Reserve Officer Training Corps. Most people called the Corps ROTC.

Colin was intrigued, and he joined the ROTC. He recalled later how he felt when he first put on the brown and olive-green uniform. "The uniform gave me a sense of belonging," he said. Suddenly he became one of 1,500 ROTC students on the CCNY campus. He joined an ROTC society called the Pershing Rifles. He began looking forward to the drills and military classes. He learned how to read maps and shoot a rifle. He also learned about basic infantry tactics and army procedures. In the summer, he attended ROTC camps.

For Colin, there was a lot to like about ROTC. "I found a selflessness within our ranks that reminded me of the caring atmosphere within my family," he said. "Race, color, background, income meant nothing. If this was what soldiering was all about, then maybe I wanted to be a soldier."

ROTC members stand at attention during a flag ceremony.

ROTC became Colin's focus during his college years. He made many friends. He even helped recruit other students into ROTC. When he graduated from City College in 1958, he had a C average and a degree in geology. More importantly, he had earned straight A's in ROTC and was named the Distinguished Military Graduate for his class.

This was important. Normally, ROTC graduates receive Army Reserve commissions. Colin received a standard commission. On June 30, 1958, he became a second lieutenant in the United States Army. His first assignment was basic training at Fort Benning, Georgia.

He said goodbye to his parents and boarded a bus for Georgia. His parents expected he would fulfill his three-year commitment to the Army and then return home. They did not consider a military career a "real" job. They also believed that had he not joined the Army voluntarily, the Army would have drafted him to serve.

Colin trained at Fort Benning for five months. He was an infantry officer now. Infantry members fight on foot. They must learn how to use weapons and perform hand-to-hand combat. He ran obstacle courses in the hot, humid Georgia summer. He hiked at night for miles guided only by a compass.

Recruits scramble over an obstacle course at an Army training base.

Army troops during ranger and airborne training exercises.

Next for Colin was ranger and airborne training. He learned how to jump from an airplane and immediately be ready to fight. He also practiced surviving the worst possible battlefield conditions. He and his colleagues would march all night through snake-infested swamps. They carried 50-pound (23-kg) packs on their backs. Even when the training seemed so hard no one could make it, Colin was ready with a smile or joke.

Colin was well prepared for his training. He was not prepared for the racism he found in Georgia. Georgia in the 1950s and 1960s was segregated. Segregation is when white and black people have separate facilities, such as restaurants, restrooms, and churches. Colin had grown up around people of many different colors. His sister had married a white man. There was none of that in Georgia. "I could go into Woolworth's and buy anything I wanted, as long as I did not try to eat there," he said.

Fortunately, the Army base was not segregated. On base, Colin could socialize with people of all races. It was another reminder of the unique brotherhood of soldiers that had first attracted him. "I did not feel inferior, and I was not going to let anyone make me believe that I was."

Hot Seat, Cold War

Colin finished his training in January 1958. His first assignment came that October. He transferred to West Germany, where he commanded a platoon of 40 soldiers. His outpost was on the border of West Germany and the Soviet Union. At that time, the United States was deep in a Cold War with the Soviets. Colin's platoon's job was to alert the Army if it appeared the Soviets were getting ready to attack.

During his two-year command, Colin was promoted to first lieutenant. In November 1960, he was sent back to the United States. His new assignment was Fort Devens, Massachusetts. Fort Devens was within driving distance of New York City, and Colin missed his family. He looked forward to being able to see them again.

Fort Devens also was within an hour of Boston, Massachusetts. Many of the soldiers went to Boston for weekend leave. Colin was no exception.

Standing behind a barbed-wire barricade, East German children look across the border into West Berlin, Germany.

One day in November 1961, Colin went to Boston for a blind date. His blind date was with the the roommate of a woman dating a friend of Colin's. Her name was Alma Johnson, and she was from Birmingham, Alabama. She was attending graduate school in audiology, learning how to teach people who have problems hearing.

The date went so well that Colin and Alma went on a second date. And a third. And a fourth. Alma later said that the dashing young officer was "probably the nicest person I had ever met."

The young people's families had reservations about the couple. Alma came from a family with a strong background in education and business. They felt a military career was a step below them. Colin's family was concerned that Alma was from a family of Southern African Americans. They felt Southern African Americans were very different from African Americans who came from the West Indies as they had.

Fate stepped in that summer. The Army promoted Colin to captain in June. In July, he learned his next assignment would take him to a small country in central Asia. It was called Vietnam, and it was in the midst of a civil war. Unlike in West Germany, this assignment would involve real shooting.

Colin Powell with his wife Alma in 1994.

Colin was excited about the new assignment. Alma was not. Colin also realized he didn't want to lose Alma by going to war. They were married in Birmingham on August 25, 1962.

Colin's family traveled from New York to attend the big wedding. They were concerned about visiting Birmingham, however. Racial tensions in the city and throughout the South had begun to increase. More and more people of color were refusing to be treated like second-class citizens. At the same time, many whites did not want to see anything change. The result was anger on both sides.

In December 1962, Colin left for Vietnam. Alma moved back to live with her parents in Birmingham. She was now expecting her and Colin's first child. As it turned out, both she and Colin would be living in a war zone in the coming year.

Tour of Duty

*F*ew people had even heard of Vietnam in the early 1960s. For years, France had ruled the southeastern Asian country. In 1954, an army of soldiers led by a man named Ho Chi Minh defeated the French. Ho Chi Minh believed in communism. Communism is a system of government where the state, or country, controls important functions like manufacturing and transportation.

Representatives from the Community Army and the French government met in Switzerland to decide what to do next. They divided the country in two at the 17th parallel. North of the 17th parallel, North Vietnam had a communist government. South Vietnam kept its old government.

By 1958, the two Vietnams were fighting each other. Communist supporters in South Vietnam, called the Viet Cong, wanted to unite the entire country under communist rule. The government of South Vietnam did not want communist rule. The result was civil war.

An Army patrol in South Vietnam.

Shortly after their wedding, the Powells transferred to Fort Bragg, North Carolina. Colin took a six-week training session to become a military adviser. He then left to be an adviser to the government of South Vietnam.

The South Vietnamese government was called the Army of the Republic of Vietnam, or ARVN. Colin was sent to a mountainous region of South Vietnam near the border of Laos. There he and 11,000 other American soldiers worked with ARVN soldiers.

Sometimes their "advising" was more a matter of common sense. Once he explained to the ARVN commander that he could save soldiers' lives if he had them wear bullet-proof vests. Another time he found them cutting down trees by shooting at them. He explained that the bullets they were using cost eight cents each. They could use saws instead for free.

Still, the assignment was very dangerous. The conflict in Vietnam was unlike previous wars involving American soldiers. It was an irregular, or guerrilla, war. The Viet Cong frequently hid and ambushed American and ARVN troops. Colin lost many of the soldiers in his unit to Viet Cong snipers hiding in the jungle.

The Viet Cong also set booby traps for their enemies. Colin was on patrol with his soldiers one day when he stepped on a punji stick the Viet Cong had placed in a hole in the ground. The sharpened stick penetrated the sole of his boot and punctured him. To make matters worse, the Viet Cong had dipped the tip of the stick in animal dung, which caused a bacterial infection in the wound.

Colin was taken back to the South Vietnamese capitol of Saigon for treatment. Unlike many others in Vietnam, he fully recovered. Shortly after that, his yearlong tour of duty was over, and the Army sent him back to the United States. There he finally was able to meet his new son, Michael, who had been born while he was away.

Wounded soldiers are evacuated from a battlefield in Vietnam.

War at Home

 C olin returned home to a nation in its own kind of civil war. The civil rights movement had begun in earnest. Martin Luther King, Jr., had called for equality between African Americans and whites. Violence between whites and African Americans had escalated. While Colin was gone, Alma had heard gunfire many times in Birmingham. Sometimes her father had to keep watch at night with a shotgun in his arms.

Colin found the struggle disturbing on many levels. He himself had been denied service at restaurants because of his color. He also knew that there were many African Americans fighting in Vietnam. It seemed as though some people thought African Americans were equals when it came to going to war. But away from the battlefield, they were not.

Following Vietnam, Colin took Advanced Airborne Ranger Training at Fort Benning, Georgia. Afterwards, he and Alma finally found a house they could call their own. It was in Phenix City, Alabama. (The street the house sat on was renamed General Colin L. Powell Parkway in 1993.) A little over a year

Martin Luther King, Jr. (center) and his wife at a civil rights demonstration in Alabama.

after they moved to Phenix City, daughter Linda Powell was born.

Colin's new job was at the United States Army Infantry Board. He had to test new equipment and determine how well it worked. Next the Army sent him to train to be a company commander. Then, they honored him by asking him to return to infantry school as a teacher. Only the best officers were selected to teach.

In 1966, Colin was promoted to major and sent to the Army's Command and General Staff College, or CGSC. He trained for a year at Fort Leavenworth, Kansas. Out of a class of 1,244 students, Colin ranked second. Both Powells enjoyed Kansas. It was a welcome change from the racial violence they'd seen in the South.

Vietnam Once Again

*I*n June 1968, Colin was sent back to Vietnam. This time he joined the American Division as battalion executive officer. He made sure the division troops had the ammunition, fuel, and other support they needed. Then U.S. Army General Charles Gettys learned that the CGSC's second-ranking graduate was in Vietnam. He requested Colin join him as one of his staff officers.

Shortly after his transfer, Colin and General Gettys were among soldiers flying in a helicopter when it hit a tree and crashed in the jungle. Colin freed himself from the tangled, smoking wreckage. He and several other nearby soldiers risked their lives by going back to save the others who had been in the helicopter, including General Gettys. The Army awarded Colin the Soldier's Medal for his bravery and quick-thinking.

During his second tour of duty in Vietnam, Colin Powell was in a helicopter crash. He risked his life to save several men from the wreckage, including General Charles Gettys.

Protesters hold a large peace sign at a demonstration in Washington, D.C.

Colin's second tour in Vietnam ended in 1969. As a husband and father, he was glad to be going home. As an officer, he was concerned. Back in the United States, there was little support for the war— or for the people fighting it. Even the soldiers in Vietnam weren't sure what they were fighting for.

Colin felt the military had failed in supporting the people who fought the war in Vietnam. He commended the veterans, who had returned to shame and silence instead of honor and parades. "These were good men," he said. "They were no less brave or skilled, but by this time in the war, they lacked inspiration and a sense of purpose."

General Colin Powell

White House Wisdom

*B*ack in the United States, Colin was reunited with his family. Alma and their two children had lived with her parents during Colin's second tour of duty. Now the family moved to a suburb of Washington, D.C. There, Colin attended George Washington University. The Army had sent him back to school for a Master's degree in Business Administration.

For two years, the Powells lived much like any other American family. They added a second daughter, Annemarie, to their family. They became active in a local church. Colin was promoted to lieutenant colonel. He earned his MBA, and then worked for a short time at the Pentagon.

It was a tough time to be in the military. The war in Vietnam had focused attention and criticism on the U.S. military.

The White House rests under a full moon in Washington, D.C. The Washington Monument looms in the background.

Colin had to admit that some of the criticisms against the military were valid. When the Army asked Colin to apply to become a White House Fellow, he jumped at the chance.

The yearlong White House fellowship offered people the chance to work in the executive branch of the government at a senior level. It was an outstanding opportunity to hone leadership skills. More than 1,000 people applied for 17 positions. After a lengthy application process, Colin received one of them.

Colin's fellowship was in the White House Office of Management and Budget, or OMB. It is the office that sets the federal budget. At the time, a man named Caspar Weinberger headed it.

The fellowship was an exciting one for Colin. He had his first taste of political life in Washington, D.C. He learned how the federal budget was put together. He learned how to reconcile differences and handle conflicts. It was a year that would change his life.

Caspar Weinberger, Colin Powell's former boss at the White House Office of Management and Budget.

Beefing Up the "Bucs"

*F*ollowing his fellowship, Colin was ready to get back to the Army. "I had been away from real soldiering for over three years," he said. "The Army was my life." He was sent to Korea to command a battalion known as "the Bucs." The Bucs had been stationed in Korea since the Korean War in 1950-53. The battalion had fallen victim to low morale and behavior problems. Colin's job was to whip them back into shape. Sadly, he had to leave Alma and his children, ages 10, 8, and 3, for a year.

It had been 20 years since there had been a war in Korea. The soldiers serving there were simply bored. They had little to do but get in trouble. Colin quickly went to work. "I threw the bums out of the Army, and put the drug users in jail," he said. "The rest we ran four miles every morning, and by night they were too tired to get into trouble."

When his job in Korea was done, Colin returned to the United States. It was November 1974. For a time, he went back to the Pentagon. Then a new

A member of the U.S. Army talks with a South Korean soldier during a joint South Korean/U.S. training exercise.

opportunity presented itself. Colin's talents had again brought him to the attention of the Army brass. This time they sent him to the National War College.

The National War College is the highest educational institution of the U.S. armed forces. An officer must attend it if he or she hopes to become a general. Students learn the philosophy and strategy of war.

Colin brought his experiences in Vietnam to his studies at the War College. He learned how wars should and should not be fought. He studied one theory that made particular sense to him. It stated that a successful war requires three things. First, the soldiers must be professional. Second, the people must understand the goals of the war. Finally, the people must support those goals. It was clear to Colin that the last two requirements were not met during the war in Vietnam.

While at War College, Colin was promoted to colonel. After graduation, the Army sent him to Fort Campbell, Kentucky. His commander there had nothing but praise for the new colonel. "Colin was the best brigade commander we had. He was best in his tactical knowledge, in his feel for soldiers, and his ability to communicate."

In 1979, the Powells returned to Washington, D.C. Colin was going back to the Pentagon. He was promoted to brigadier general there. He took more jobs in the field in the following years, commanding battalions at Fort Carson, Colorado, and then again at Fort Leavenworth, Kansas. While at Fort Leavenworth, he started a campaign to honor the African American soldiers who fought in the Native American wars. Years later, his work would be rewarded with a monument to these brave "Buffalo Soldiers," as they were known.

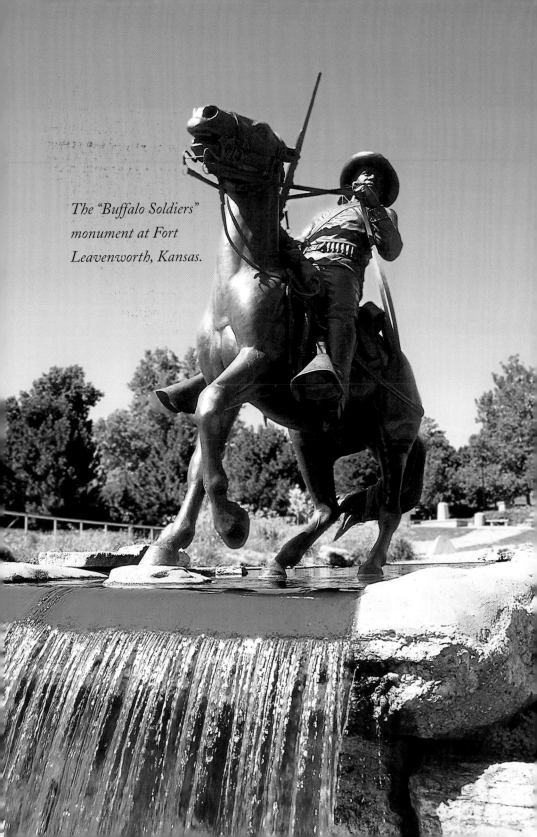

The "Buffalo Soldiers" monument at Fort Leavenworth, Kansas.

Scandal

*I*n 1983, Colin received an important call from an old OMB friend–Caspar Weinberger. Weinberger was now secretary of defense working for President Ronald Reagan. Weinberger was looking for someone to be his military assistant. He wanted to know if Colin was interested.

Colin hesitated. Outside of the military, he had less authority and responsibility. He wasn't sure he was right for a job as a Washington, D.C. political insider. However, he was loyal to Weinberger, and he finally agreed to take the job. As Weinberger's assistant, he would monitor incoming information and alert the secretary to anything he felt needed his attention.

He also would serve as a liaison between the White House and the military. When the White House had a crisis that required military assistance, they would call Colin. Such a call came in 1983 when the United States invaded the small Caribbean island of Grenada. Colin oversaw the successful U.S. invasion of the island, which happened because of a hostile military takeover.

In June 1985, Colin received a memo that eventually rocked the nation. The memo suggested that the United States sell weapons to Iran. This same nation had held more than 60 Americans hostage just a few years before. However, the people backing the plan thought Iran would be more likely to deal favorably with the United States if they could get this kind of assistance. Colin quickly took the memo to Weinberger. They did not agree with the plan. However, their jobs bound them to pass the memo to the Defense Department.

Colin Powell

Colin was highly effective at his White House job. However, he still yearned for the Army. He said the Army was where he felt most comfortable. He felt he did his best work as a soldier.

He got his wish in June 1986. The Army gave him command of more than 70,000 troops in Frankfurt, West Germany. He also received his second star and became a lieutenant general. For Colin, it was one of the happiest times in his life thus far.

That happiness was short-lived. By now, the United States public and Congress had learned of the plan to sell weapons to Iran. People also learned the profits from the arms sales had been used to finance the Contras in Nicaragua. The Contras were an armed guerilla force. They wanted to overthrow the Nicaraguan government, which was then led by the communist Sandinistas. Even Colin had not been aware of this. It is illegal to sell arms to another country without the approval of Congress. Congress had never been asked for its approval. Congressional leaders quickly launched an investigation.

That November, another old friend from the OMB, Frank Carlucci, was appointed national security adviser. He immediately called Colin in Germany. He wanted him to come back to the United States to be his deputy. Colin refused. He was happy where he was. Several days later, the phone

President Ronald Reagan

rang again. This time it was President Ronald Reagan asking Colin to come help. Colin's code of honor would not allow him to refuse the president. "Mr. President," he said, "I'm a soldier, and if I can help, I'll come."

As a deputy to the national security advisor, Colin had to advise both Carlucci and the president on when to use the military to resolve conflicts. He also had to warn them what the effects of using the military would be. Colin's experiences in Vietnam had prepared him well for the role.

He was not, however, prepared for the firestorm of the Iran-Contra investigation, as it came to be known. Both Colin and Weinberger had to testify about their role. Colin knew he had acted with integrity. Not everyone saw things the same way, however. He quickly learned to appear cool and in control when in front of the news media.

Family Tragedy

Colin and Alma had only recently returned to Washington, D.C., when they learned their son Michael had been in an accident. Michael, who had joined the Army, had been stationed in West Germany. He had been a passenger in a jeep when the driver lost control. The jeep flipped and Michael was badly injured.

Michael nearly died. The doctors said he might be in a wheelchair the rest of his life. He was flown back to a hospital in the United States. After surgery, he was able to come to the Powell family home. He endured painful therapy sessions every day. After a year and a half, he was able to walk with a cane. Yet his career as a soldier was over. Colin was proud of his son for fighting and winning such a horrible battle. He ended up graduating from law school and getting a job at the Pentagon

Colin Powell

By this time, Colin was in charge of the National Security Council. His assignment was among the toughest he'd ever faced. The Council was embroiled in the Iran-Contra controversy. Colin took charge, rebuilt the morale of the department and faced tough questions from reporters head on. It was no surprise President Reagan asked him to be his national security adviser in November 1987. Colin became the first African American to serve in that position.

It was an exciting time to be national security adviser. Communism in the Soviet Union was crumbling under Mikhail Gorbachev. Colin was heavily involved in negotiating arms reductions with this new Soviet Union.

In 1988, George Bush was elected president. Colin was not as close to Bush as he had been to Reagan. He was surprised in October 1989 when Bush picked him to be Chairman of the Joint Chiefs of Staff.

The Joint Chiefs of Staff is a military advisory group to the president and the secretary of defense. It includes the Army and Air Force chiefs of staff, the Navy's chief of naval operations, and the commandant of the Marine Corps.

General Colin Powell, Chairman of the Joint Chiefs of Staff.

Colin was by now a four-star general, but he was younger than the other contenders for the job. Not only was he the first African American to serve in the position, at age 52, he also was the youngest.

Colin's skills were put to the test almost immediately. At that time, Panama was a political hot spot because of its military ruler, Manuel Noriega. Colin remembered the lessons of Vietnam. He urged President Bush to use enough military force to remove the leader quickly and effectively. Operation Just Cause invaded Panama in December 1989 with the largest U.S. military force since Vietnam. The brief operation was mostly successful.

Then in August 1990, the Iraqi army invaded Kuwait. Iraq claimed that it owned Kuwait. The United Nations disagreed and called for an economic embargo, which prohibited countries from buying and selling things to Iraq. When the embargo still did not force Iraq out of Kuwait, the United Nations approved using force.

The White House looked to Colin for direction. "When we go to war, we should have a purpose that our people understand and support," he said. He spent the fall of 1990 educating Congress on how best to handle the conflict.

Colin Powell was the first African American to serve as Chairman of the Joint Chiefs of Staff. At age 52, he was also the youngest person to fill the position.

*Allied jets patrol the skies
during Desert Storm.*

Congress approved Operation Desert Storm in January 1991. Colin tapped another Vietnam veteran, General Norman Schwarzkopf, to command the U.S. forces. Desert Storm pummeled Iraq with bombing raids for a month, then finished the job with ground forces. By the end of February, Kuwait had been freed.

Colin continued as Chairman of the Joint Chiefs until his second term ended in 1993. The president by then was Bill Clinton. Colin and Clinton did not agree on many issues involving the military. Colin knew Clinton would seek another chairman for the Joint Chiefs. He decided to retire from the Army. Those who knew him well knew he wasn't truly retiring. He was just switching jobs.

Colin Powell visits an Army camp during the Gulf War.

A Vision For Youth

*F*or Colin, retirement meant more time with family. He was now a grandfather thanks to his son Michael. His daughter Linda had finished college and was pursuing a career in acting. His youngest, Annemarie, also had graduated from college and was working as a journalist.

In 1995, Colin started a new chapter in life—literally. He published his autobiography *My American Journey*. He took on speaking engagements around the nation. And, like his wife Alma had been doing for years, he began to volunteer.

In February 1997, he announced he was forming America's Promise—a national campaign to help young people. The program reaches out to young people at risk of falling victim to drug abuse, violence, and teen pregnancy. It helps them get the skills and support they need in life to succeed.

Secretary of State
Colin Powell

When forming the organization, Colin made a simple request. He asked that "every single person who has been successful give some of their time, talent, and money to help a child in need." He put extra firepower behind that request. He spent two years traveling the country asking for commitments of time and money.

Colin also "adopted" Macfarland High School in Washington, D.C. He made frequent visits to the primarily African-American and Hispanic school to talk with students. He also was instrumental in refurbishing the school library.

Today, Colin Powell has his hands full as secretary of state. That position makes him fourth in the line of succession to the presidency.

On September 11, 2001, New York City's World Trade Center and the Pentagon in Washington, D.C., were attacked by terrorists, who used jumbo jets as weapons of destruction. Thousands of innocent people died in the attacks. Secretary of State Powell immediately sprang into action, using all his years of military and diplomatic experience to bring together the countries of the world in order to fight terrorism.

In press conferences after the attack, Powell said, "We are very grateful for the resolution that has come from the Senate and the support that the Congress is giving to our efforts. It shows the United States as a

Colin Powell listens as President Bush talks to the National Security Council after the September 11, 2001, terrorist attacks.

nation, as a people, coming together in this time of crisis, and showing our determination to move forward deliberately and decisively to deal with this particular incident, as well as the broader threat represented by world terrorism... Leaders around the world want to work with the U.S.—not only in the specific case of what happened September 11, but in response to the general recognition that terrorism is a crime against all civilization."

In the years to come, it's possible that Colin Powell will be asked once again to run for president. What he does is anyone's guess. What is likely, however, is that he'll do what he needs to do to serve the country he loves.

Timeline

April 5, 1937: Colin Powell born in Harlem, NY.

1958: After participating in the Army Reserve Officer Training Corps (ROTC), receives commission from U.S. Army as a second lieutenant upon graduating from City College of New York.

1962-63, 1968-69: Serves two tours of duty in Vietnam.

1972: Selected as a White House Fellow.

1987-1989: Serves as Assistant to the President for National Security Affairs.

1989-1993: President George Bush selects General Powell to become Chairman of the Joint Chiefs of Staff.

1990-91: Oversees military command of Gulf War.

1995: Publishes autobiography, *My American Journey.*

2001: Becomes first African-American secretary of state under President George W. Bush.

Where on the Web?

http://www.state.gov/secretary/
A biography from the United States Department of State web site.

http://www.shider.com/history/ powell.htm
A biography of Colin Powell. Lists awards and honors, both civilian and military.

http://www.armyrotc.com/
The U.S. Army ROTC home page.

http://www.historyplace.com/ unitedstates/vietnam/
A history of the Vietnam War, in words and pictures.

http://www.pbs.org/wgbh/pages/ frontline/gulf/
An online version of PBS's Frontline history of the Gulf War.

Glossary

ambush
When an enemy hides so it can conduct a surprise attack.

cabinet
The top advisers to the president.

Civil Rights Movement
The struggle to gain full citizenship rights for African Americans.

Cold War
A conflict where each side stops just short of military action.

communism
The concept or system of society in which the major resources and means of production are owned by the community instead of individuals.

Contras
Guerilla opposition forces who opposed the communist Sandinista government of Nicaragua.

infantry

The part of the military that moves and fights on the ground.

Joint Chiefs of Staff

The military advisory group to the president and the secretary of defense. It includes the Army and Air Force chiefs of staff, the Navy's chief of naval operations, and the commandant of the Marine Corp.

National Security Council

Advises the president about domestic, foreign, and military policies affecting national security. Members include the president, vice president, and secretaries of state and defense.

Pentagon

The headquarters of the Department of Defense.

Racism

Discrimination against someone based on the belief that their race is inferior to another.

segregation

To keep people of different races separate.

Index